July

To Euge...

Best wishes

from,

Monica & John.

(Come and see it for yourself)

AUSTRALIA
COLOURFUL CONTINENT

AUSTRALIA
COLOURFUL CONTINENT
IRENE DAVEY/MICHAEL MORCOMBE

THE SNOWY MOUNTAINS, NEW SOUTH WALES
A late afternoon sun casts blue shadows across the heavily forested gorges of the Snowy Mountains near Cabramurra. In the far distance can be seen the waters of Talbingo Reservoir, part of the Snowy Mountains Hydro-electric Scheme, situated on the Tumut River. A few miles eastwards of this high lookout point, on the road which crosses the Snowy Mountains from Adaminaby to Khancoban, reaching altitudes of more than 5,000 feet, is Kiandra, a gold-rush town of the 1890s and today a winter sports centre.

RIGBY

RIGBY PUBLISHERS LIMITED • ADELAIDE
SYDNEY • MELBOURNE • BRISBANE
NEW YORK • LONDON
First published 1972
Reprinted 1975
Reprinted 1980
Copyright © 1972 Irene and Michael Morcombe
ISBN 0 85179 460 2
Photographs on pages 23, 36, 63, 127 copyright Jocelyn Burt
Photographs on pages 10, 17, 44, 46, 50–51, 64, 100, 101,
108, 110, 111 copyright Keith P. Phillips
Wholly designed and set up in Australia
Printed in Hong Kong

Contents

1 Coastline   Page 7

2 Desert   29

3 Mountains   43

4 Rivers and Waterfalls   59

5 Lakes   71

6 Plains   79

7 Canyons and Gorges   87

8 Trees and Forests   103

9 Unique Features   113

10 Changed by Man   121

I Coastline

Where sea meets land around Australia can be found some of this continent's most fascinating scenery. Here more than anywhere else is a world of changing moods, ranging from sparkling azure-blue sunlit waters of tropical seas around coral reefs, or golden sunrises and red sunsets reflecting on gleaming wet sand, to scenes of dark low clouds, howling wind, and thundering breakers.

Some parts of the coastline are remote, rugged, almost inaccessible, and seldom seen except by the most adventurous. These would include the magnificent island-studded Kimberley coastline, the mangrove-fringed shores of the Gulf of Carpentaria and Cape York, and the shores of south-western Tasmania where deep inlets are overshadowed by snow-capped mountains.

In many other places, particularly in southern Australia, the shores are easily reached by road. In some places these coasts are a scenic attraction: the high cliffs at Port Campbell, at Royal National Park near Sydney, and at Point Labatt in South Australia. The grand scale of the view across to Hinchinbrook Island in north Queensland, the massive headlands and hills at Rocky Cape in Tasmania, and Victoria's Great Ocean Road coastline—these are places that can hold a spectator spellbound.

Elsewhere again along Australian shores are gentler scenes—beaches ideal for surfing and fishing, as found at Wilson's Promontory in Victoria, and at Two People Bay in south-western Australia.

The Australian coastline and its immediate hinterland has a wonderful variety of plant, bird, and animal life. On Tasmania's eastern coast is an extensive shallow expanse of water known as Moulting Lagoon. Here the Black Swans renew their feathers, returning in their thousands every year for this purpose. Some of Western Australia's most valuable wildlife sanctuaries are the small islands of the Abrolhos group, and the Shark Bay islands, where sea birds nest in huge numbers, and the population of small animals are safe from extermination by cats and foxes.

South Australia has at Point Labatt, on Eyre Peninsula, Australia's only mainland colony of Sea Lions, and at Port Campbell in Victoria the high rocky islets are safe Mutton-bird breeding grounds.

The islands and reefs along the Queensland coast comprise some of Australia's richest coastal environment. Many offshore islands have tropical rainforest, while the shallow waters of the reefs are famed for their corals and colourful sea creatures.

PORT CAMPBELL COASTLINE, VICTORIA
The south-eastern coast of Victoria in the vicinity of Port Campbell is one of Australia's most forbidding, with miles of almost unbroken cliffs undercut in places to form arches, canyons, and blowholes. Residual spires make fortress-like islands along the coast. Some of these are the breeding grounds for Mutton-birds (Short-tailed Shearwaters).

NOOSA HEADS, QUEENSLAND
Sunrise across the Pacific at Noosa, southern Queensland, turns the beach sands golden, while grotesque pandanus palms in the foreground remain black silhouettes. Noosa is a small national park about 100 miles north of Brisbane. Above these beaches and headlands its higher parts are forested, with pockets of rainforest in the gullies, while on its southern slopes and coast are wildflower heathlands. A few miles north are the famed coloured sands of Cooloola, a popular tourist attraction but now in danger of being mined. Cooloola has coastal wallum country and rainforests, and represents a unique type of coastal environment worthy of preservation.

Above:
TWO PEOPLE BAY, WESTERN AUSTRALIA
This deep bay on the south coast is sheltered to the west by a granite-domed headland which, with adjacent coastal sandplains, forms a reserve for the rare Noisy Scrub Bird. It was at the foot of Mount Gardner (background in this scene) that the Scrub Bird was sighted in 1961, for the first time since 1889. Other pairs were later found to have territories in the low dense scrub on the slopes of Mount Gardner. In the foreground are the rocky shores of another rugged peninsula which includes Mount Manypeaks, where the small carnivorous marsupial Antechinus apicalis, commonly called Dibbler or speckled pouch mouse, was rediscovered in 1967. This beautiful coastline is relatively untouched by development, and its heathlands have an exceptional variety of wildflowers through spring, summer, and autumn.

Left:
THE SENTINELS, SOUTH-WESTERN VICTORIA
Rocky residuals like spires rising high above churning seas form some of the finest coastal scenery in south-eastern Australia. Here, 160 miles south-west of Melbourne, between Cape Otway and Warrnambool, the huge wave-cut cliffs of the Port Campbell coastline claimed many sailing ships. One of these nineteenth century wrecks was the Loch Ard, which went down near a forbidding chasm now known as the Loch Ard Gorge.

Above:
FISHERMAN, WHISKY BAY, VICTORIA
Whisky Bay, on the western coast of popular Wilson's Promontory, is a smooth sweep of beach between huge tumbled piles of boulders. Holiday times bring crowds to this national park, one of Victoria's largest. Here they can follow a variety of outdoor activities, as energetic as bushwalking or as relaxed as fishing from a secluded beach while the sun dips below the western horizon.

Right:
THE CERVANTES ISLANDS, WESTERN AUSTRALIA
Along Australia's western coast, north of Perth, are many small islands set in azure seas and surrounded by extensive reefs. Most have been sculptured from jagged limestone, with many wave-cut caves, ledges, and crevices. Rarely visited except by fishermen, these islands are safe nesting grounds for a great many sea birds; in this photograph an old Osprey nest can be seen on the highest rocky corner of the island.

Left:
BRUNY ISLAND, TASMANIA
On Tasmania's Bruny Island is spectacular coastal scenery of cliffs
and bold headlands jutting into the sea, while its enclosed bays offer
safe anchorage for small craft. Forests and fern gullies cover inland
parts. Bruny Island is a long, irregular-shaped land mass sheltering
the estuary of the Huon River south of Hobart. A vehicular ferry makes
several trips daily on summer and winter schedules, running between
Kettering, twenty-three miles south of Hobart, and Barnes Bay on the
island.

Above:
HINCHINBROOK ISLAND, NORTH QUEENSLAND
*Rising high above tidal flats and mangrove swamps, cloud-capped
Hinchinbrook Island is best seen from Highway One just north of
Ingham. Except for a small picnic area situated by a sandy beach near
fresh water at The Haven, this rugged jungle-covered island with peaks
almost 4,000 feet high remains a magnificent wilderness, as yet
undamaged by man.*

15

Left:
WILSON'S PROMONTORY, VICTORIA
A mountainous, wild, desolate headland thrusting deep into the waters of Bass Strait, Wilson's Promontory is connected to the mainland by a low strip of sand. The promontory has much attractive scenery, with granite-domed hills and deep verdant gullies. From these hills are breathtaking views of precipitous granite headlands, sweeping white beaches, and numerous small offshore islands. The Tidal River camping area serves as a base with walking tracks leading to such beauty spots as Sealers Cove, Refuge Cove, Waterloo Bay, and the Lighthouse.

Above:
STRIKING COAST FORMATION, SELLICK'S BEACH, SOUTH AUSTRALIA
This colourful formation of rocks is part of the 500-mile arc of hills in South Australia, extending from Kangaroo Island, northwards through the Mount Lofty Ranges to the Flinders Ranges. The well-rounded hills of this extension of the Mount Lofty Ranges near Sellick's Beach indicates the great age of the ranges, while the colourful and contorted cliff sections are comparatively young. Sellick's Beach is located thirty miles south of Adelaide, and is one of several south coast beaches becoming increasingly popular for their surf.

Left:

WILDFLOWERS ON COASTAL CLIFFS NEAR SYDNEY,
NEW SOUTH WALES

Ten miles of the Pacific coast, with high cliffs and dramatic headlands broken here and there by fine surf beaches, forms the eastern boundary of popular Royal National Park, only twenty miles from the heart of Sydney. As well as ocean beaches there are sheltered waters where the sea has penetrated between steep forested hills of the lower reaches of the Hacking River. Here the natural bushland provides a sanctuary for several hundred species of birds, some seven hundred different wildflowers, and many native mammals.

Above:

EAGLEHAWK NECK, TASMANIA

Across this stormy bay on the eastern side of Eaglehawk Neck is a rocky headland, whose seaward side has high cliffs and awe-inspiring chasms known as the Devil's Kitchen, Tasman's Arch, and The Blowhole. Eaglehawk Neck itself, in the immediate foreground, is a narrow low sandy strip of land connecting Tasman Peninsula to the Tasmanian mainland. In convict days savage dogs were tethered across this narrow strip of land as a deterrent to escapees from Port Arthur, twelve miles further south.

19

Left:
CAPE LEEUWIN, WESTERN AUSTRALIA
Breakers of the Indian Ocean thunder against half-submerged boulders
at Cape Leeuwin, Western Australia's extreme south-western corner.
On a high narrow headland overlooking this scene stands a tall stone
lighthouse, and nearby an ancient waterwheel. Five miles away the
small town of Augusta, one of the oldest settlements in the state, is
now a popular summer holiday and tourist resort.

Above:
POINT LABATT, SOUTH AUSTRALIA
The white limestone cliffs of Point Labatt overlook small beaches
sheltered by flat ledges and reefs extending seawards. It is on these
beaches and rocks that Australia's only mainland colony of sea lions
are found. Here seals bask lazily on beaches and flat rocks, each
massive bull accompanied by his "harem" of half a dozen or more
smaller females. Point Labatt is approximately twenty-three miles
south of Streaky Bay, on the western coast of Eyre Peninsula.

Above:
THE ISLAND ARCH AT PORT CAMPBELL, VICTORIA
The high limestone cliffs near Port Campbell are being carved away by the ocean at a comparatively fast rate, leaving harder portions standing as small islets. Pounding at the base of one such residual the sea has broken through to form this huge island archway 100 feet or more in height. Elsewhere along the twenty miles of cliffs are the London Bridge, an archway attached to the mainland, and the Blowhole, where the sea surges underground for a quarter of a mile, to reappear in the depths of an enormous vertical blowhole shaft.

Above:
THE GREAT OCEAN ROAD, LORNE, VICTORIA
Where the high forested ridges of the Otway Ranges fall steeply to the ocean, a road has been carved into the slopes just above the water, winding around each headland and bay to reach the small resort town of Lorne. Although parts of the ranges have been heavily exploited for timber, this area still contains some of the most beautiful coastal scenery within easy reach of Melbourne.

Above:
NORMAN BAY, VICTORIA
From a clear sky the late afternoon sun highlights the sparkling surf, gleaming sand, and small tidal pools between boulders on the long beach of Norman Bay, Wilson's Promontory. This is probably the best-known of the promontory's beaches; its wide sweep of pure white sand extends more than a mile between two high sheltering headlands. Nearby is the national park's Tidal River camping area, popular resort for thousands of Victorians.

Right:
ROCKY CAPE, TASMANIA
With its succession of massive orange-coloured headlands and rocky bays, the Cape juts into Bass Strait 104 miles west of Launceston, on Tasmania's northern coast. Of special interest are the large caves between Rocky Cape and Table Cape. It is thought that these were formed by the pounding of the waves when the sea was up to 100 feet above its present level more than 250,000 years ago. The caves are unique and valuable areas for archaeological research, as they contain shell middens left by the now extinct Tasmanian Aborigines.

SUNRISE OVER BARRIER REEF ISLANDS,
QUEENSLAND

*From the heights of forested hills above Shute
Harbour in Conway National Park extends a
panorama of islands which, for a few minutes
at sunrise, seem set in a sea of molten gold.
As the sun rises higher the true colours will be
revealed—blue-greens of luxuriant tropical
vegetation, emerald greens of shallow water
over coral reefs, and the azure blue of the sea,
with here and there a line of white sandy
beach. Many of these islands are mountainous,
particularly the larger islands along Whit-
sunday Passage. Their forests are a refuge for
a great variety of creatures, including the
Brush Turkey.*

2 Desert

Australia's deserts constitute by far the largest of the major natural environments of the continent. Dryness dominates all but the coastal fringes; the heart of Australia is a vast expanse of arid and semi-arid terrain stretching from the Great Sandy Desert's Eighty Mile Beach in north-western Australia, across the scrub and spinifex of the Tanami Desert, to the forbidding sand dunes of the Simpson Desert.

In a north-south direction it is more than a thousand miles from the northern fringe of the desert, southwards through the Great Victorian Desert, to the coastal cliffs of the Nullarbor, where the desert comes right to the sea. In an east-west direction deserts extend more than fifteen hundred miles from western New South Wales to the dry north-western Australian coast.

The vast central desert touches upon all States except Tasmania, and takes in the greater part of the Northern Territory. All of Western Australia is desert or very dry except the south-western corner and the Kimberley; most of South Australia north of the Flinders is arid; dry country touches upon north-western Victoria, and takes in much of western New South Wales and western Queensland.

Within this enormous area of arid and semi-arid land are situated many scenically spectacular places, some well known, others still relatively secluded and as yet completely unspoiled.

The Australian desert country is a world of red plains and red sand dunes, distant purple ranges, fiery red gorges, dry claypans, and glaring white salt lakes. Unexpected and refreshing contrast is provided by the lush greenery of river gums and in places even palms around river pools and waterholes, as in Palm Valley in central Australia.

The Australian deserts and their dry fringes fall between the tropical and the Antarctic rainbearing wind systems, and receive some rain (but very little) from both north and south. The rain which does reach the Centre tends to come in sudden deluges and thunderstorms. These may send water flooding down the gorges, fill the salt lakes, and turn roads into impassable quagmires. But such a flood may be the last good rain for a year, two years, or even five years.

Over the ages this area has become progressively more arid, so that its flora and fauna has become steadily better adapted to survive the rigours of the harsh climate. This is a region of tremendous botanical and zoological interest, and depending upon rain, or the lack of it, the interior can be a "living desert" or a hot barren dusty wasteland.

THE PINNACLES, WESTERN AUSTRALIA
Near the sandy windswept western coast north of Perth is a strange region known as the Pinnacles Desert. This desert is a result of natural wind erosion, exposing thousands of limestone spires of varied colour, size, shape, and texture. In some places the vegetation has reclaimed the dunes, and weathered pinnacles stand among trees, blackboys, and low coastal scrub.

Left:
SPINIFEX RANGE COUNTRY NEAR MOUNT HERBERT,
WESTERN AUSTRALIA
From the summit of Mount Herbert (100 miles east of Derby), the brown and red iron ore ridges, their rugged surfaces only partly hidden by the golden spinifex, extend to the horizon. Although such north-west country may seem barren and devoid of wildlife, it has its own special creatures, such as the rufous-crowned Emu-wrens, with incredibly long emu-feather pattern tails on tiny brown and blue bodies, living in the harsh spinifex clumps.

Above:
SAND DUNES AT EUCLA, NULLARBOR PLAINS,
WESTERN AUSTRALIA
For the Nullarbor traveller, arrival at old Eucla is indicated by the sighting of dazzling white sand dunes far away on the southern horizon. The present-day Eucla, which caters for the needs of the overland traveller, is now at the top of Eucla Pass, but Eucla as originally established in 1877 was right on the shores of the Great Australian Bight. Today the old ruins can still be seen half-buried by the advancing sand. Eucla was built as a link in the overland telegraph line between Perth and Adelaide, but with later re-routing of the line along the Transcontinental Railway, the telegraph station was closed and the buildings abandoned, eventually to be engulfed by the wind-blown sand.

DUNE LANDSCAPE, THE PINNACLES,
WESTERN AUSTRALIA

*Moving sand-drifts continuously cover and
uncover tombstone-like rocks and here and
there the remains of a stunted tree. The wind
has rippled the sand surface, and gouged
hollows where it swirls around each limestone
rock. Newly uncovered pinnacles have a
variety of colours, from orange-brown to
white, but in other nearby areas where the sand
has long been stabilised by vegetation the stone
has become grey and weathered. The Pinnacles, now a part of Nambung National Park,
are about 120 miles north of Perth.*

Right:
WOORAMEL RIVER CLIFFS, WESTERN AUSTRALIA
Red rock, red earth, distant purple ranges, and sparse stunted mulga scrub could be said to be typical of vast areas of northern Western Australia. The dark shadowed cliffs mark the course of the Wooramel River. At this point, where it is crossed by the Mullewa-Gascoyne Junction road, the Wooramel is about 100 miles inland from Shark Bay, where it finally meets the Indian Ocean. The river here is, for most of the year, a chain of pools. Some are very beautiful in their setting, lying behind rock bars that at intervals cross the sandy river bed.

Above:
GIBBER STONE DESERT, NORTH WESTERN AUSTRALIA
Where harsh desert conditions of extreme heat and cold, prolonged droughts and eroding deluges have removed the soil, only gleaming gibber-stones cover the plains. Polished by wind-blown sand the stones, large and small, rounded or angular in shape, represent almost all that remains of the ancient land surface. They may be red, brown black, or translucent quartz, but when seen against the light they all glitter like mirrors scattered across the plains.

Above:
COOPER'S CREEK GIBBER COUNTRY, SOUTH AUSTRALIA
Cooper's Creek and its tributary the Diamantina drain a huge area of country noted for its erratic rainfall, the years of drought or low rainfall being broken occasionally by torrential downpours. It is then that Cooper's Creek comes down in flood. In this harsh environment the soil in many places, unprotected by vegetation, has washed and blown away, leaving only the countless gibber stones.

Right:
DESERT OAK, NORTHERN TERRITORY
Westwards from Alice Springs towards Ayers Rock the track passes red desert sand dunes, with here and there the beautiful Desert Oaks, a species of Casuarina. In the years of good winter rains, the red clay flats where the Desert Oaks grow between the parallel sand ridges will be carpeted with wildflowers through August and September.

Above:
NEAR THE SIMPSON DESERT, NORTHERN TERRITORY
Flowering in massed profusion beneath rugged hills at the western edge of the Simpson Desert, desert everlastings appear in such numbers only on rare occasions when sufficiently heavy rains have penetrated so far inland. These papery flowers, Myiocephalus stuartii, *are known as Poached-egg Daisies. Each flat flower head is actually made up of a dense cluster of tiny yellow flowers surrounded by an encircling ring of white bracts. This scene is on the old road along the railway, not far south of Alice Springs.*

Right:
WILDFLOWERS AT MOUNT OLGA, NORTHERN TERRITORY
In early spring wildflowers appear on the clay flats around the base of Mount Olga, gaining extra water from the run-off from the bare rock. This species is the Tall Yellowtop, Senecio magnificus, *a tall robust perennial plant up to three feet high, with stout stems and large composite flower heads.*

DESERT SALT-LAKE AND CLAY-PAN, WESTERN AUSTRALIA

By far the greatest part of the Australian environment consists of deserts and their arid and semi-arid fringes — yet maps show lakes scattered through the driest parts. These almost without exception are salt lakes or claypans, dry except after rare heavy rains. When water does flood into these depressions the surrounding saltbush flats and mulga scrub become alive with wildlife, including Orange Chats, Crimson Chats, and Emus. A trail of footprints has been left by an Emu crossing the deep mud of this salt lake near Yalgoo.

3 Mountains

Australia's mountains are small by comparison with those of other continents, but encompass a tremendous variety of scenery. Many of our mountains are no more than ranges of hills. But on a landscape as flat as that found over most of Australia, hills which rise suddenly from level plains have a visual impact far greater than their modest altitude suggests.

This is particularly true of some of the central Australian ranges, where rough rocky hills, with very little vegetation to hide the raw earth colours of their cliffs and gorges, are visible from a great distance across the flat mulga-scrub plains. At first they are seen as purplish-blue silhouettes rising above the horizon, then, closer, in rich colourings with deep blue shadows in the gorges and steep valleys.

Australia's principal region of mountains is in the south-east, including Tasmania. Here are situated the only snowfields, and the only alpine flora. The central Tasmanian highlands have almost perennial snows, at least on the higher peaks, and the flora is distinctly alpine. Imposing mountain peaks are almost too numerous to mention. Some of the best are those through the Cradle Mountain and Lake St Clair National Park, and Frenchman's Cap, where huge vertical cliffs provide a real mountain climbing challenge.

On the mainland, the Australian Alps and Snowy Mountains have some of the finest and most extensive snowfields. This great mountain fastness of weathered snow-bound rock outcrops, alpine plateau, and steep, forested ridges is best known as a winter playground. But it is just as fascinating in summer when thousands of visitors tour the alpine highways, fish for trout in cold clear mountain streams, and hike or ride across the high plains.

The alpine vegetation of the south-east and Tasmania has its own spectrum of wildflowers —Snow Daisies, Alpine Sundews, Mountain Gentians, Alpine Podolepsis, and many others. The fauna includes rare creatures found only on the mountain tops, such as the Corroboree Frog, as well as many birds which visit the high plains in summer.

There are many high ranges in other parts of the continent, such as the jungle-clad 5,000 feet Mount Bartle Frere of north Queensland, unique within Australia for its combination of tropical rainforest and high altitude. In the interior are the Hamersleys and the Mac-Donnells. New South Wales has its Warrumbungle Range with volcanic spires and knife-like ridges; and in south-western Australia is the abrupt, jagged Stirling Range, famed for its endemic wildflowers.

BELOUGERY SPIRE, WARRUMBUNGLE RANGE, NEW SOUTH WALES
The Warrumbungles, a jagged outcrop of volcanic domes, spires, and ridges, are the result of volcanic eruptions about 13 million years ago. This range has been described as the "place where east meets west." Although it is situated on the comparatively dry inland plains, it has forested, damp, and shady gullies which provide a habitat more like that of the coastal ranges.

Above:
SOUTHERN WALLS OF WILPENA POUND, SOUTH AUSTRALIA
From Moralana a superb view extends across gently rolling hills with scattered native pines to the distant reddish and purplish cliffs of Wilpena Pound. Wilpena is a huge natural amphitheatre in the Flinders Ranges; a broad basin enclosed within a continuous ring of hills, the inward slopes of which rise gradually to heights of 3,800 feet, then fall in precipitous cliffs right around the outer perimeter. The only easy access is through a narrow gorge on the east side, through which flows the Wilpena Creek.

Right:
THE NEEDLES, GIBRALTAR RANGE, NEW SOUTH WALES
These huge rock spires rising high above the precipitous jungle-clad eastern escarpment of the New England Tableland are known as The Needles. They are included in the Gibraltar Range National Park, accessible by a five mile walking track through eucalypt forest and rainforest country, where Lyrebirds, Scrub Turkeys, Potoroos, and other wildlife can be seen. Gibraltar Range is located approximately mid-way between Grafton and Glen Innes on the Gwydir Highway.

Left:
COLOURFUL CREED BED, FLINDERS RANGES,
SOUTH AUSTRALIA
Between the many hills that together make up the Flinders Ranges are countless watercourses, mostly dry except immediately after rain. From gorges in the higher, more rugged parts the creeks break out on to the flats and meander between more gently sloping foothills. The Flinders Ranges creeks, lined with gnarled old River Red Gums, have a certain uniformity of appearance. Devoid of any screening or protecting small bushes or undergrowth after so many of years of heavy grazing, the richly-coloured, deeply-eroded creek banks are a distinctive part of the Flinders scene.

Above:
CASTLE-LIKE LIMESTONE TOWER, CHILLAGOE,
NORTH QUEENSLAND
Formed a great many millions of years ago as part of a chain of coral reefs, this castle-like tower, one of many in the Chillagoe district, rises abuptly several hundred feet above the surrounding plains. The dark grey limestone is streaked here and there with brighter orange and reddish markings, while the jagged tops have the appearance of castle battlements. Below ground level the limestone contains many beautiful caves, some with stalactite and other formations in colours ranging from pure white to rich red-brown. Several caves, designated national park areas, can be visited on guided tours.

Above:
THE BLUE MOUNTAINS, NEW SOUTH WALES
The Blue Mountains are famed for the misty blue colours of the distant vistas from their higher cliff-top lookouts. For many years the Blue Mountains were an impassable barrier to the westward expansion of settlement until 1813, when Blaxland, Lawson, and Wentworth successfully planned their route along the flat-topped ridges. Today the railway and the Western Highway follow this route closely. The Blue Mountains National Park is forty miles west of Sydney. High vantage points are reached by cars, but the terrain of deep forested valleys and narrow gorges makes access possible only to skilled bushwalkers and rock climbers, except where paths and steps have been constructed.

Right:
STIRLING RANGE, WESTERN AUSTRALIA
A remarkable range of jagged peaks, not particularly high, but rising so suddenly from the flat plains that they look more like a true mountain range than almost any other hills in Australia. Situated close to the south coast of Western Australia, the summits of the Stirling Range are often covered in cloud, which creates cool humid conditions. This has permitted the survival or evolution of unique wildflowers such as the Mountain Bells that are to be found on one peak or another.

48

THE BREADKNIFE, WARRUMBUNGLE
RANGE, NEW SOUTH WALES
*One of the strangest formations of the volcanic
Warrumbungle Range is the high natural rock
wall known as The Breadknife, from its roughly
serrated outline. Molten magma was forced into
a deep fissure in the volcano's cone and solidified.
Since it is extremely hard it has defied the erosion
which has over millions of years stripped away
the surrounding rock debris and soil. Today the
lava wall, cracked into huge blocks, stands 300
feet high, but in places measures no more than
five or six feet in thickness. In the surrounding
hills are many other tall spires and rocky hilltops
formed by the same volcanoes long ago.*

SUMMER WILDFLOWERS, MOUNT KOSCIUSKO,
NEW SOUTH WALES
*As the deep snowdrifts on the slopes of the Snowy Mountains melt
from late November to January, the alpine wildflowers appear; a few
at first, then spreading until they almost cover parts of the swampy
valleys. These alpine buttercups,* Ranunclus gunnianus, *like other
mountain wildflowers, are adapted to withstand the harsh winter
conditions when they are buried under many feet of snow.*

Above:
MISTY JUNGLE GORGES, ATHERTON TABLELAND,
NORTH QUEENSLAND
*Mount Bartle Frere, highest mountain in Queensland, looms above
the misty jungles of the Atherton Tableland and the gorges of the
Johnston River. These north Queensland jungles are the greatest belt
of tropical rainforest in Australia. They contain the richest and most
fascinating of Australia's fauna. Hidden in their green twilight are
such creatures as the tree kangaroo, the twenty-foot-long Scrub
Python, the Cassowary, Golden Bowerbird, Prince Albert Riflebird,
huge bright butterflies, and tropical orchids.*

55

CREEK-BED GUMS NEAR WILPENA,
FLINDERS RANGES, SOUTH AUSTRALIA
*Framed by the arching limbs and fresh green
foliage of River Red Gums the Flinders Ranges,
blue with the haze of distance, rise to heights of
almost 4,000 feet. The Flinders countryside, for
most of the year a scene of golden browns and
yellows of earth and dried grass, and red, tan, and
purplish strata of rock on the cliffs of the ranges,
becomes refreshingly green after the first winter
rains. This country is best seen from July to
September, avoiding the summer months of heat
and dust.*

4 Rivers and Waterfalls

Australian rivers and waterfalls are as varied in their setting as they are in size and volume of water. The rivers encompass every mood, from crystal clear icy cold mountain creeks trickling from melting snowdrifts, to the broad muddy estuaries and tidal lower reaches of major waterways such as the Murray, which drains almost one-quarter of the continent.

On many of the Australian rivers it is probably in the lower reaches, where the water flows so slowly that its movement can hardly be detected, and there are wide flood-plains and reed-filled billabongs, that the greatest variety of animal life is to be found. This includes the water birds—ducks, swans, and pelicans on the open waters, herons and egrets wading along the shores, ibis on the grassy flats, and bitterns, crakes, and swamp-hens among the reeds. The lower reaches of the coastal tropical rivers also have such occupants as fresh-water and salt-water crocodiles.

The rivers of the drier parts of inland Australia have a totally different character. Most of the year they are no more than chains of pools beneath high banks and spreading eucalypts. The surrounding country has usually a dry and desolate appearance, with low mulga scrub and scattered, stunted gums. The sparse vegetation does little to screen the rich red and yellow ochre colours of the rock and clay of the river banks, which together with the reflected blues and greens of sky and tree-top foliage make many scenes of colourful beauty along the rivers of the far inland.

But this peaceful scene can change completely when a tropical cyclone swings down across the northern coast, bringing floods which break over the banks and spread miles wide each side of the main river channel.

On a continent so largely arid the rivers which flow through semi-desert country are particularly valuable as fauna habitats; their pools provide water for birds and mammals, while the riverside gums, often the only large trees for many miles, are nest sites for many species of birds.

Almost all of Australia's waterfalls are on rivers of the coastal mountain ranges of eastern and south-eastern Australia, and Tasmania. Although very few are noteworthy for their size, many are set in natural environs of considerable scenic beauty, like the tropical rainforest surrounds of Wallacha and Nandroya Falls, and the tree-fern gully of Russell Falls.

SNOWY RIVER HEADWATERS, MOUNT KOSCIUSKO, NEW SOUTH WALES
As the snowdrifts melt through spring and summer, crystal clear, icy cold mountain streams tumble from the alpine highlands. This little stream, sparkling over polished boulders between banks of hard-packed snow, is one of innumerable similar mountain creeks feeding the Snowy River, which eventually reaches the coast near Orbost, Victoria.

Above:
RUSSELL FALLS, TASMANIA
Set among huge Mountain Ash trees, Russell Falls is a beautiful symmetrical series of cascades where a crystal-clear mountain stream tumbles 120 feet in two sheer drops into a cool moist gorge, and flows away between high mossy banks and beneath the lacework canopy of tall tree-ferns. Russell Falls are on the lower slopes of Mount Field, a mountainous plateau rising to 4,721 feet, and situated fifty-two miles north-west of Hobart.

Right:
MILLSTREAM FALLS, NORTH QUEENSLAND
One of Australia's widest waterfalls, with a total breadth of 200 feet, Millstream is situated on a tributary of the Herbert River, in open woodland country on the western slopes of the Atherton Tableland. The falls, which have a vertical drop of approximately sixty feet, are divided into two parts by an island in the centre of the stream. The waters divide just before plunging over the cliff, and reunite downstream as they tumble away over small cataracts and polished boulders.

Left:

WOORAMEL RIVER, WESTERN AUSTRALIA
Picturesque Wooramel River crosses the north-west coastal highway south of Carnarvon, where its floodwaters have several times destroyed the high-level bridge. Approximately 100 miles inland the Wooramel flows across the north-south Mullewa-Gascoyne Junction road, where a low-level crossing becomes impassable when the river rises. This scene, near the river-bed crossing, shows the Wooramel as it is for most of the year—a shallow stream connecting long placid pools that reflect sky, trees, and the colourful high river banks.

Above:

SUNRISE ON THE MURRAY, MANNUM, SOUTH AUSTRALIA
Mannum, forty-two miles by road east of Adelaide, was the launching place of the first Murray River paddle steamer. The river was once a major transport route, with numerous steamers plying from South Australia up-river to Albury. Today the only remaining paddle steamers are tourist attractions, relics of a past era. The Murray is in many places still a very beautiful river, with its old overhanging gums silhouetted against broad still reaches of silvery water, and the distant misty line of trees and reedbeds of the opposite banks.

Above:
AUTUMN ALONG THE MITTA MITTA RIVER, VICTORIA
Golden autumn foliage on poplar trees along the banks of the Mitta Mitta makes an effective colour contrast against the blue-grey of distant ranges. The Mitta Mitta River has its headwaters between the summits of Mount Bogong (6,516 feet) and Mount Hotham (6,101 feet) in north-eastern Victoria. It flows at first in a south-easterly direction as it tumbles down the mountain gorges, then curves towards the north, until its course is north-westwards across flat flood plains of broad valleys. From between these gently rounded hills the Mitta Mitta flows finally into the Hume Reservoir, to join the Murray at Albury.

Above:
WALLACHA FALLS, NORTH QUEENSLAND
*In the semi-darkness of a luxuriant Queensland jungle, Wallacha
Falls drop from a rocky river bed and a preceding series of small
cataracts, down over a wide undercut precipice to a deep pool,
among treeferns, palms, and other tropical vegetation. Wallacha
Falls are situated between Innisfail and the Atherton Tableland, and
may be reached by a half-mile walking track from the Palmerston
Highway.*

65

Left:
FINKE RIVER IN ORMISTON GORGE, NORTHERN
TERRITORY
*Cutting through the MacDonnell Ranges almost under the shadows
of the cliffs of Mount Sonder, this tributary of the Finke River drains
a huge rock-walled basin known as Ormiston Pound. The river's
gorge here is impressive, with high cliffs of rich and in places fiery
colours, ranging from deep burnt tones to rust, vermillion, dazzling
white, and yellow, with occasional veins of grey and coal black.
Vegetation in these ranges is very sparse—a smudge of harsh yellow-
green spinifex on the stony heights, with an occasional Ghost Gum;
River Gums along the watercourses; and mulga scrub across the
plains.*

Above:
MURCHISON RIVER, WESTERN AUSTRALIA
*Two hundred miles inland from its coastal gorges the Murchison
River flows through semi-arid scrub country. Its permanent tree-
lined pools are an attraction for wildlife from many miles around,
particularly in spring when parrots, cockatoos, hawks, and many
other birds come to nest in the only large trees across many miles of
plains. Australia's inland rivers, though they flow only after good
rains, often contain permanent waterholes, or water hidden beneath
their sandy beds.*

67

Above:
TROPICAL WATERCOURSE, NORTH KIMBERLEY,
WESTERN AUSTRALIA
*North of the rugged King Leopold Ranges the Kimberley landscape
is principally of extremely rough ranges, interspersed with plains and
valleys. Among these hills are innumerable waterfalls, fed by heavy
summer monsoonal rains. In places the rivers and creeks run between
banks lined with the bright green pandanus palms that are so typical
of wet tropical regions. It is here, amid lush greenery, that the character
of Australia's far northern waterways is most distinctive compared
with southern and inland rivers.*

Right:
DESERT WATERCOURSE, INLAND WESTERN AUSTRALIA
*Good rains, sufficient to start creeks and rivers flowing, are of infre-
quent occurrence in the dry north of Western Australia. For months,
sometimes years, there is not a pool to be found for many miles along
the beds of even the largest rivers. In this harsh stony region the only
trees are these red-barked mulgas, a tough species of Acacia that can
survive even where no eucalypt finds sustenance. In this scene, a few
weeks after cyclonic rains, pools still remain in a small rocky watercourse, reflecting the grotesque beauty of the tough red desert mulgas.*

5 Lakes

Like her rivers and waterfalls, Australia's lakes are not noteworthy for size, nor are they common features of this largely dry continent. But scattered across Australia in settings ranging from mountain valleys to desert plains are some lakes of outstanding scenic beauty.

On maps of Australia there are shown many lakes, some of huge size, in the desert and semi-desert interior. Almost without exception these are dry salt lakes; some, like Lake Moore in Western Australia, are apparently the remains of ancient rivers that flowed in the distant past when these regions were far more humid than today. South Australia's Lake Eyre, with an area of 3,600 square miles, is perhaps the best known. On the rare occasions when Cooper's Creek and the Diamantina flood, their waters can transform this lake's flat bed of clay and white salt into a vast inland sea.

A complete contrast to the dead lakes of the desert country are the glacial lakes of Tasmania and the south-eastern mountains. A huge sheet of ice, which covered central and south-western Tasmania to depths as great as 1,000 feet, rounded the summits of hills with its slow grinding movement, and gouged deep valleys from solid rock. Great piles of stones were dropped across the valley floors as the ice melted, building moraines that dammed rivers and created the many exceptionally beautiful lakes that are a feature of the Tasmanian landscape today.

Lake Dove and Crater Lake occupy deep cirques cut into the sides of Cradle Mountain; the Great Lake of the central highlands and Lake St Clair are also attributed to the periods of glaciation. Lake St Clair, lying between mountain peaks, is 720 feet deep, ten miles long and three to four miles across.

Mainland Australia too has its mountain-top lakes; best known are Lake Cootapatamba, just below the summit of Mount Kosciusko, at an altitude of 6,800 feet, and nearby Lake Albina, at 6,340 feet.

Tropical Australia is not without its lakes. Among the most interesting of these are the "crater lakes" of the Atherton Tableland, which lie in craters formed by volcanic explosions. Both lakes are surrounded by luxuriant tropical rainforest, and their clear waters are tremendously deep—480 feet to the bottom of Lake Eacham, and 360 feet for Lake Barrine.

LAKE DOVE, TASMANIAN HIGHLANDS
Lake Dove reflects a magnificent mountain landscape that changes hour by hour, day by day, season by season. The lake may be mirror smooth, reflecting every detail, or ruffled by winds, breaking the image into patterns of colour; the sky may be clear, then within a short time the mountain capped with threatening clouds; the surrounding alpine heathlands may display a profusion of wildflowers, or be buried beneath feet of snow.

Above:

RESERVOIR, DARLING RANGE, WESTERN
AUSTRALIA

*Bleached skeletons of tall forest trees are mirrored
across the surface of a small reservoir in the hills
near Dwellingup, about fifty miles south-east of
Perth. This small earth-walled dam has been built
across a valley of the Darling Range, in the heart
of the Jarrah forest country. This eucalypt, which
gives an extremely hard and durable timber,
covers more than 3 million acres in the south-
west of Western Australia.*

Top right:
MOUNT KOSCIUSKO, SNOWY MOUNTAINS
*Summer snowdrifts on a southern slope almost at
the summit of Mount Kosciusko overlook little
Lake Cootapatamba. Though best known for its
extensive winter snowfields, this mountainous
region in south-eastern Australia is in many ways
more interesting in summer.*

Bottom right:
LAKE ST CLAIR, TASMANIA
*Nestling between mountain peaks, Lake St Clair
occupies a long, narrow, and very deep basin
gouged from solid rock by a glacier, during an ice
age in the distant past. The lake is 2,419 feet above
the sea level, eight miles long, one mile wide, and
more than 700 feet deep. Rising above the forested
lower slopes of Mount Olympus (4,746 feet) on
the left, is the rocky summit of Mount Ida.*

LAKE DOVE AND CRADLE MOUNTAIN, TASMANIAN HIGHLANDS

Situated in the mountainous heart of Tasmania, Cradle Mountain's well-known jagged outline is reflected in the glassy waters of Lake Dove. Although it is late summer, a patch of snow still clings to the side of the mountain. This is a region of rough open moorland and windswept heaths, broken by deep gorges and forested valleys in which lie numerous lakes and countless small tarns of great beauty. Vegetation on the highest areas is treeless alpine moorland. Forests of ancient mossy Antarctic Beech trees, temperate rainforests and eucalypt forests grow at lower altitudes. On boulders around the lake can be seen the deep striations gouged by the moving ice which carved out the basin now occupied by Lake Dove.

Above:
ALPINE LAKE, HARTZ MOUNTAIN, TASMANIA
Hartz Mountain is situated in the extreme south of Tasmania, south-west of Geeveston. The glacier-carved summit is the remains of an old plateau surface; rising to 4,113 feet, it is covered with snow for the greater part of the year. Near the summit, almost at the upper limit of tree growth, are several small lakes, around which stand the bleached white stumps of many trees which have succumbed to the extremely rigorous winter climate.

Right:
LAKE JANDAKOT, NEAR PERTH, WESTERN AUSTRALIA·
The water of this small shallow lake on the Swan Coastal Plain south of Perth has a strange sepia colour, most noticeable in the shallows where the bottom is white sand. This colour is possibly organic in origin, as there are extensive reedbeds around the shores. In this scene the water laps around the roots of a twisted old banksia tree; in the reeds is a large Swamp Sheoak.

6 *Plains*

Australia, the flattest continent on earth, is more than anything else a land of plains. Its mountains are no more than a ridge of coastal ranges rarely exceeding 5,000 feet in height, while the occasional inland range that reaches similar heights is generally only a few thousand feet above the level of the surrounding plateau top.

Plains dominate the Australian landscape in most regions. The western half of Australia is a tableland averaging around 1,000 feet above sea level. Its gently undulating surface forms plains that stretch unbroken for many hundreds of miles, and are then separated only by low ranges from further wide plains.

At the southern edge of this plateau is a perfectly flat expanse of limestone plain, entirely treeless over much of its area. This plain, the Nullarbor, has porous underlying rock, with caves and blowholes, into which all surface water rapidly disappears.

There are also very extensive plains across tropical northern Australia, from the Kimberley through the Tanami Desert and the Top End of the Northern Territory to the almost-treeless Barkly Tableland of north-western Queensland. In all that great distance only the rough ranges of the north Kimberley, and of Arnhem Land, break the flatness of the grassland plains. Here, on the coastal Northern Territory river plains, is the most abundant wildlife to be found on plains country anywhere in Australia.

Large areas of the northern grasslands have scattered trees, creating a parkland effect, a type of vegetation known as savannah-woodland. In some places where there are few trees, tall tower-like termite mounds occur in great numbers, and completely dominate the landscape.

To the east are the plains of the Murray-Darling basin. Much of this is black-soil country, in some parts covered with eucalypt woodlands, and elsewhere carrying extensive grasslands or saltbush.

In both eastern and western Australia there are lowland plains between the ranges and the sea. These are some of the best-watered and most fertile lands on the continent—but for this very reason have suffered the greatest alteration at the hands of man. There now remains very little to see of the original natural scenery of the coastal lowlands except in parts remote from heavy population, or where national parks have been established. Here, such plants and animals as have not completely vanished cling to a greatly diminished natural environment.

WILDFLOWERS ACROSS THE PLAINS,
NORTHERN TERRITORY
East of Alice Springs the MacDonnell Ranges are comprised of a series of parallel east-west ridges interspersed with wide flat plains. For most of the year, and sometimes for years unbroken, the ground here is almost bare except for an occasional Ghost Gum and scattered low shrubs, but these low papery wildflowers carpet the plains in amazing profusion after winter rains.

Above:
MULGA-SCRUB PLAINS, WESTERN AUSTRALIA
Seen from the flat-topped Kennedy Range, the featureless mulga-scrub plains of northern Western Australia extend to the horizon, where both plains and ranges are lost in the haze of distance. These inland plains are used for grazing sheep, but in many parts over-stocking, particularly in times of drought, has led to the disappearance of many of the small shrubs that once grew between the scattered mulga trees. This part of the Kennedy Range and adjacent plains was once the Merlinleigh sheep station; it has long been abandoned, with only a few ruined buildings, rusting windmills, and broken fences as evidence of pioneering hopes and labour.

Right:
PARAKEELYA ON INLAND PLAINS, WESTERN AUSTRALIA
Stark dead mulga trees among the stunted scrub of the inland plains reveal the effect of frequent and prolonged drought; the carpet of wildflowers is but a transient splash of colour, lasting but a few weeks in early spring. These are a species of Calandrinia, commonly known as Parakeelya. By their water-storage ability these plants are well adapted for survival in arid regions.

TERMITE-NEST TOWERS, NORTHERN TERRITORY

Reaching heights as great as twenty feet, the columnar termite mounds of Australia's tropical northern grassland and savannah-woodland country are cities of insect activity, sometimes built with what seems almost scientific understanding of climatic conditions. Some species of termite build their towers with wide thin buttresses which face the morning and evening sun with their broadest surfaces, and present a narrow edge to the hot mid-day sun, thereby controlling temperature within the termite mound. The humid warmth of the termite mounds attracts other creatures. Several species of parrots and kingfishers dig nest tunnels into termite mounds, while large goannas scratch into the lower part to bury their eggs which become sealed within the mound in ideal warm moist conditions.

Left:
LAKE MOORE, WESTERN AUSTRALIA
From the summit of Mount Singleton extends a panoramic view across seemingly endless plains. Lake Moore, a vast maze of shallow saltpans which probably were part of a large river system in the distant past when rainfall was far greater than today, meanders across the flats until lost in the heat haze towards the far horizon. Mount Singleton, a rocky, scrub-covered hill, is situated north-east of Wubin, inland from the north-eastern extremity of Western Australia's wheat farming belt.

Above:
WILDFLOWERS ON ABANDONED FARMLANDS,
WESTERN AUSTRALIA
Wildflowers flourish where crops failed many years ago on these inland plains of Western Australia. Rusted machinery and broken fences remain as evidence that there was once an attempt to cultivate in this arid region. Today a few stunted shrubs have appeared across the paddocks, but regrowth of native vegetation has been extremely slow. Only in early spring, if there have been adequate rains, is the hard bare ground covered, at first by the green of the newly germinated annuals, then by massed papery flowers.

85

7 Canyons and Gorges

In many parts of Australia, steep-sided chasms, cut by running water into the sides of ranges and tablelands, contain spectacular scenery. Between their rocky walls is a closer, more intimate landscape. Panoramic views and distant vistas are replaced by the colour and texture of rock. There is the awe-inspiring grandeur of vertical walls rising hundreds of feet overhead on both sides; the ever-changing patterns of sunlight and shadow across sculptured cliffs; the shaded damp luxuriance of vegetation in the depths of a gorge, even in desert country; the fascinating reflections in pools; and the mysterious Aboriginal paintings and engravings in caves and on the walls of overhanging cliffs.

Some of the largest and most beautiful gorges in Australia are those of the far north, in the rugged Kimberley region of Western Australia and the tropical Top End of the Northern Territory.

About seventy miles east of Derby the narrow three-mile-long Winjina Gorge cuts through the Napier Range. Some three hundred million years ago this abrupt wall of limestone was a coral reef comparable to the Great Barrier Reef. The vertical walls of Winjina Gorge, weathered grey but streaked here and there with red-brown and yellow ochre tones, rise to jagged battlement-like tops. The still river pools reflect this rather forbidding yet very beautiful scene.

Towards the Top End of the Northern Territory is one of the most spectacular of all Australian river gorges, the Katherine. Here are high red cliffs, dropping vertically to very deep water. But it is the river itself that makes Katherine Gorge so breathtakingly beautiful. In the breathless calm of a hot day it mirrors the whole scene of colourful cliffs, trees, and sky. An occasional puff of wind sends gentle ripples across the surface to break these images into abstract patterns of colour.

One of the most interesting of the gorges of eastern Australia is a tremendously deep chasm cut into the Carnarvon Ranges, in Queensland. Gouged from white sandstone, Carnarvon Gorge is twenty miles long, up to six hundred feet deep, and varies from a few yards to a mile in width. In its shadowed depths are rare ferns, Aboriginal rock carvings and paintings.

There are many other canyons and gorges around Australia: the colourful gorges of the Flinders Ranges in South Australia; the fiery-coloured canyons of central Australia; Western Australia's fifty-mile long Murchison River Gorge; the brick-red and golden gorges of the Hamersley Ranges; and the steep-sided yet forested gorges of the Australian Alps and the Tasmanian highlands.

TOURIST BOAT IN KATHERINE GORGE,
NORTHERN TERRITORY
A tourist boat, seen from the top of the very high vertical cliffs of Katherine Gorge, ripples the deep river pool of one of the most spectacular scenic attractions of the Northern Territory. The pools are interrupted in several places by rock bars. Here visitors must walk around the section of rapids before continuing upstream in boats kept on the next long pool.

Above:
RIVER GORGE, KALBARRI, WESTERN AUSTRALIA
The Murchison River of Western Australia has carved a tortuously winding course to reach the Indian Ocean. Near the coast, just inland from the small resort town of Kalbarri, it has eroded fifty miles of meandering gorges hundreds of feet in depth, through variously coloured sandstone, creating multi-coloured cliffs horizontally banded in white, yellow, and red.

Right:
GORGE IN CAPE RANGE, WESTERN AUSTRALIA
North West Cape juts into the Indian Ocean at the north-western corner of Western Australia between Carnarvon and Onslow. The cape has a central ridge of extremely rugged hills, which were once relatively flat-topped, but have over the ages become deeply dissected by a great many precipitous gorges, making a landscape resembling the Blue Mountains of New South Wales.

Above:
ZIG-ZAG GORGE, MURCHISON RIVER,
WESTERN AUSTRALIA
In the Zig-zag Gorge in Kalbarri National Park the effects of colour, light, and shadow vary greatly according to the angle of sunlight across each cliff face. Above the river gorge are extensive sandplains, with low heath vegetation that carries a magnificent display of wildflowers in spring and early summer.

Top right:
WINJINA GORGE, FAR NORTHERN
WESTERN AUSTRALIA
Where the Lennard River cuts through the Napier Range, in the West Kimberley district, a huge gorge, with cliffs several hundred feet high, has been formed. This limestone range was once a coral reef in a primeval ocean, but now crosses the flat plains like huge walls. Winjina Gorge was once known as Devil's Pass because of the strange Aboriginal paintings in the area.

Bottom right:
GEIKIE GORGE, TROPICAL WESTERN
AUSTRALIA
The huge Fitzroy River has cut a long winding gorge through craggy limestone at the junction of the Oscar and the Geikie Ranges, ten miles from the small Kimberley town of Fitzroy Crossing. Geikie, now a national park, is a major northern tourist attraction. The deep long river pools remain right through the dry season, and contain fresh-water crocodiles, barramundi, and other water creatures.

Above:
GLEN HELEN, FINKE RIVER, NORTHERN TERRITORY
A shallow pool of the Finke River at the entrance of Glen Helen Gorge reflects reds of cliffs and hills, and the blue of clear Australian sky. This is a well-known tourist area eighty-one miles west of Alice Springs, close to Mount Sonder and Ormiston Gorge. The Finke is the largest river of the MacDonnell Ranges; most of the canyons and gorges in these ranges to the west of Alice Springs have been made by this river and its tributaries.

Right:
KATHERINE GORGE, NORTHERN TERRITORY
In parts of Katherine Gorge the cliffs overhang almost to the extent of forming caves, into which it is possible to row a small boat on clear water so deep that the bottom cannot be seen. Looking out from a rowing boat in such a cave one sees the colourful cliffs framed by the black sides and ceiling, while the small waves rippling in from the wind-riffled river reflect, in abstract patterns, all the colours of the outside scene.

KATHERINE GORGE, NORTHERN TERRITORY

In the second gorge section of Katherine Gorge the huge cliffs drop vertically into deep water along both sides, so that a boat is essential. The first section upstream from the mouth of the gorge has earth banks with trees and other vegetation. It is along these reaches of the river that fresh-water crocodiles, up to eight feet in length and becoming less wary now that this is a national park, can occasionally be seen basking on rocks just above water level. At the end of the first section visitors must walk around shallow rapids to proceed in another boat through the second gorge. Now the vertical walls of the cliffs continue downwards through crystal clear water as far as can be seen, and the gorge takes a series of sudden zig-zag turns. Here the boat intrudes into a place of superb natural scenery, enhanced, on a windless day, by reflections in the glassy water of all the colours of cliffs, trees, and sky.

Left:

KING'S CANYON, NORTHERN TERRITORY

The walls of this canyon suggest ancient ruins of enormous buildings. They are on one side smooth at the top, but lower down have a rugged masonry appearance, as if the surface rendering had fallen away over the centuries. On the other side of the canyon the cliffs overhang threateningly; on the slope below are fallen blocks of stone, some the size of a house. This is a short, dead-end canyon, with a small creek, normally dry, at the bottom. King's Canyon is situated in the George Gill Range, 230 miles west of Alice Springs.

Above:

THE MOLL GORGE, KIMBERLEY, WESTERN AUSTRALIA

North of the jagged King Leopold Range, which for a long time was a barrier to vehicular traffic into the northern Kimberley, this gorge cuts through a stony range of hills. During the summer wet season this region's heavy rainfall brings floods rushing through innumerable remote gorges such as this; but in the dry season, from April to December, their pools and shady vegetation make them a very pleasant refuge from the hot dry dusty plains.

97

Above:
DALE'S GORGE, HAMERSLEY RANGE, WESTERN AUSTRALIA
This gorge, one of the best-known of the tourist features of the Hamersleys, is approached from above. The road from Wittenoom climbs slowly through wide gorges until the plateau-like top of the range is reached. The road terminates in a seemingly featureless area, and then, unexpectedly, the gorge is seen, a tremendous chasm dropping away almost at one's feet. At the head of the gorge is a small waterfall dropping to a deep pool, from which a creek runs through dense vegetation; there are even ferns in damp places under overhanging rocks.

Right:
ORMISTON GORGE, MACDONNELL RANGES, NORTHERN TERRITORY
At Ormiston a large tributary of the Finke River has cut through a ridge of the MacDonnell Ranges almost at the foot of one of the highest peaks, Mount Sonder. The north-western wall of Ormiston Gorge is in fact the south-eastern flank of Mount Sonder, with almost vertical slopes and cliffs that must in total height rise almost 1,000 feet above the river. The opposite side has lower cliffs of deep-red rock. To see much of the gorge it is necessary to scramble through, climbing over boulders and possibly wading across the river at a shallow point.

Above:
EAST PAINTER GORGE, NORTHERN FLINDERS RANGES,
SOUTH AUSTRALIA
*The northern Flinders landscape in the Arkaroola-Mount Painter
area is extremely rugged, with sharp ridges and steep gorges alternat-
ing far into the distance. Its little-traversed regions have been one of
the last strongholds of the Yellow-footed Rock-wallaby, one of the
most attractive members of the kangaroo family. These have ridged
soles on their feet, enabling them to leap confidently from rock to
rock, and move fearlessly and swiftly along the most frightening
cliff ledges.*

Right:
NOOLDOO NOOLDOONA GORGE, NORTHERN FLINDERS,
SOUTH AUSTRALIA
*In the northern parts of the Flinders Ranges the hills become higher,
the landscape more desolate. Water flows in the creeks only inter-
mittently, although occasionally there are permanent pools in deep
shaded gorges. It is along such valleys and creek beds that the only
dense vegetation is seen. This part of the Flinders, around Arkaroola,
is becoming popular with tourists exploring beyond the well-beaten
trail; generally the best time to visit is from autumn to spring.*

8 Trees and Forests

Of the trees native to Australia, the vast majority are eucalypts, commonly known as "gums." There are more than 500 distinct species, occupying a variety of habitats from mountain-top snowfields to tropical woodlands, from river floodplains and swamps to dry stony desert ranges.

Eucalypts have the world's tallest hardwood trees, the Mountain Ash, which soars 300 feet or more into the air, and the stately Karri trees of south-western Australia, which are almost as tall.

At the opposite end of the scale are the dwarf eucalypts of the arid interior. These scrubby, drought-resistant trees may attain heights of no more than five to thirty feet, depending on the species. Some grow as bushy shrubs, while others develop the characteristic mallee habit of growth. From each large knotted rootstock just below the surface of the ground rise numerous slender stems, around which the bush debris of dead leaves, strips of bark and twigs accumulates, effectively covering the ground and conserving moisture around the roots.

Eucalypts are commonly named for their bark. Those with smooth bark are generally known as gums: for example the River Red Gum and the South Australian Blue Gum. But if there is a dark rough collar of old bark around the trunk the trees are given such names as blackbutt and woollybutt. Trees with long-fibred barks are known as stringybarks, while many other trees have their own distinctive barks—the peppermints, ironbarks, boxes, bloodwoods, and ashes.

There are many other less numerous types of trees which are of great interest—the tropical baobabs, the wattles, banksias, she-oaks, and the rainforest softwoods such as Red Cedar, Native Ash, Antarctic Beech, and Strangler Fig.

While eucalypt forests are usually dominated by a single species of tree, the rainforests of north-eastern Australia are a mixture of a great many intermingled types. They are tropical jungles, with all the steamy mossy luxuriance of ferns, vines, and arboreal orchids. There is little undergrowth in the half-darkness at forest floor level far below the dense canopy of foliage. Fallen trees soon become soft and rotten under these constantly humid warm conditions, and are covered with velvety green moss and orange fungi.

In the tropical rainforests there are unexpected glimpses of beauty—a huge clump of golden orchids on a branch of a lofty tree, or a shaft of sunlight through the translucent new red fronds of ferns. Rainforests are a rich and fascinating environment occurring in very restricted areas in Australia. These forests, especially, are in need of careful conservation.

POPLAR GUMS, NORTHERN TERRITORY
Tropical Poplar or Mottled Gums, Eucalyptus alba, *make a beautiful sight when their sunlit salmon-pink limbs are seen against a clear-blue sky. These trees will be seen along the Stuart Highway south of Darwin. This is a widespread species across northern Australia, from the Kimberley to Queensland.*

Above:
BAOBAB OR BOTTLE TREE, NORTHERN TERRITORY
These unusual trees are characteristic of far northern Australia from the Kimberley region of Western Australia through the Top End of the Northern Territory to northern Queensland. They derive their name from the bottle-like shape rather than from any water-storing ability, although it is sometimes possible to obtain water from small hollows where branches join the trunk. They are also unusual among Australian trees in that they are deciduous, dropping their leaves during the winter dry season, probably in order to conserve water.

Right:
TROPICAL RAINFOREST, NORTHERN NEW SOUTH WALES
The rainforests differ greatly in appearance and composition from other Australian forests. Huge buttressed trees with interlacing branches form an almost continuous canopy of foliage overhead. Only an occasional ray of sunlight breaks through the dense ceiling of leaves, vines, ferns, and arboreal orchids. Vegetation at ground level in a mature rainforest is usually sparse. Unlike the hardwood eucalypt forests, where one tree species dominates in a particular locality, the rainforests are composed of many species of intermingled softwood trees.

Left:
KARRI FOREST, WESTERN AUSTRALIA
In the extreme south-west corner of Western Australia are some of the tallest trees on this continent, in height second only to the Mountain Ash of the south-east. Karris, which eventually tower as much as 300 feet above the ground, are fast growing under their natural heavy rainfall conditions—during their first ten years some specimens have added five feet each year to their height. The Karris are most attractive when their normally grey-white and blue-grey bark flakes away to reveal the new pale orange-yellow bark.

Above:
BUSHFIRE IN JARRAH FOREST, WESTERN AUSTRALIA
Bushfires occur occasionally in the extensive forests on the Darling Range east and south-east of Perth. Destructive though these are, they have at times a unique beauty—at night, when fires on distant forested hills resemble city lights, or towards sunrise and sunset, when the smoke haze can create the most beautiful sunrise and sunset colours. Preventive burning, with low intensity fires lit in autumn and spring, is now used to reduce the risk of major fires.

107

Left:
TREE-FERNS IN TARRA VALLEY, VICTORIA
Tall tree ferns grow in profusion in the shaded moist Tarra Valley National Park, 130 miles south-east of Melbourne. Above the fern gully tower Mountain Ash, Beech, Sassafras, and Blackwood trees, while the ground flora includes smaller types of ferns, orchids, and in very damp parts, various fungi. This valley is a haunt of the Lyrebird, while the Koala, Platypus, Black-tailed Wallaby, and various possums and gliders occur in the vicinity.

Above:
RIVER RED GUMS, FLINDERS RANGES, SOUTH AUSTRALIA
Grotesque heavy-trunked River Red Gums in a boulder-filled creek bed near Wilpena Pound have an appearance of massive solidity. The great, wide-spreading River Gums have foliage that is a refreshing bright green, and bark that is smooth, white or greyish, usually streaked with red. This species of gum, Eucalyptus camaldulensis, normally grows only along streams which have seasonal or intermittent flows, in the drier parts of Australia.

Above:
FORESTED HILLSIDES, SNOWY MOUNTAINS,
NEW SOUTH WALES
The Snowy Mountains have a great variety of vegetation which changes according to altitude. The lower slopes support dry sclerophyll forests of Manna Gums, Peppermint, Long-leaved Box, and Red Stringbark. In areas of heavy precipitation the common trees are Ribbon-bark Gum and Eurabbie. On higher slopes are found Alpine Ash, Mountain Gum, and White Gum and above the snow line, Snow Gums.

Right:
SOUTH AUSTRALIAN BLUE GUM
This is a moderate-sized tree, usually less than 100 feet in height, growing mainly on clay soils of gently undulating hilly country. The South Australian Blue Gum, Eucalyptus leucoxylon, sometimes called Yellow Gum, sheds its bark in irregular rough oval flakes leaving the trunk and branches smooth, and mottled in yellow, white, and grey.

9 Unique Features

Australia's land mass of nearly 3 million square miles is remarkably flat—almost three-quarters averages only 1,000 feet above sea level, and only the eastern coastal highlands are really mountainous. The western third, an extensive plateau, is built of very old and hard rock. At its north-western corner it rises to a high point of 4,000 feet in the Hamersley Range. Here the millions of years of weathering have produced an eroded landscape, where water has carved gorges and deep cliff-rimmed basins, such as Python Pool, from extremely hard iron-rich rock.

Even flatter is the land from the Gulf of Carpentaria through to the Southern Ocean. These central lowlands were once under the sea, around 100 million years ago. The lack of significant mountains and other large-scale physical features, together with the sparseness of vegetation, makes the various curiosities of the landscape all the more conspicuous.

The Devil's Marbles, immense rounded granite boulders, would hardly be noticed if sited in heavy forest and undergrowth of the rugged eastern coastal ranges. But when first seen by a traveller who has driven hundreds of miles across barren, almost totally flat plains, the jumbled heaps of round boulders look enormous. Nothing higher breaks the straight line of the horizon.

These strange features of the central Australian landscape were shaped by ages of weathering. The original rock mass had three main sets of joint planes at right angles to each other, breaking the granite into rectangular blocks of varying size. Erosion, at first along the lines of the cracks, then flaking away the exposed surfaces, gradually rounded the rocks to roughly spherical shape. Softer surrounding material has been completely eroded away, leaving the boulders piled high upon each other.

Probably the best known of the unique features of Australia is Ayers Rock. This massive mound of sandstone, 1,140 feet high, is all the more impressive because it is first sighted after hundreds of miles of plains, where there is nothing taller than a Desert Oak or occasional sandhill. The smooth, monolithic shape of Ayers Rock is the result of erosion upon its almost jointless sandstone.

Before the white man came, many features of Ayers Rock were of ritual significance to the Aborigines of the area.

The incredible giant domes of Mount Olga, twenty miles west of Ayers Rock, extend about four and a half miles across the flat plains, with the highest dome rising to a height of 1,790 feet. Surrounding it are some thirty smaller domes, separated by deep ravines. Such features are of geological as well as tourist interest.

PYTHON POOL, HAMERSLEY RANGE,
WESTERN AUSTRALIA
A waterfall drops through a narrow cleft to a deep circular pool, from which a small creek flows beneath trees and shrubs. The Hamersley Range country is very harsh, arid, and rocky. Everywhere the rock is deep red to chocolate brown, and sometimes almost black. It is rich in iron.

Left:
WILDFLOWERS AT MOUNT OLGA, NORTHERN TERRITORY
*Mount Olga, Mount Connor, and Ayres Rock, all within 100 miles
of each other, and all rising abruptly from the flat plains between the
Musgrave and MacDonnell Ranges, are the most striking and best
known features of central Australia. These Minuria flowers, clustered
on low bushy shrubs, grow around the base of one of the rock domes
of Mount Olga, where they benefit from the run-off after any light
rains.*

Above:
MOUNT OLGA, NORTHERN TERRITORY
*Red sandhills across the twenty miles of arid plains between Ayres
Rock and Mount Olga provide occasional high vantage points, giving
a view across the intervening low bushes and scattered Desert Oaks.
In the far distance, still some miles away in this telephoto shot, Mount
Olga's red sandstone rock has a hazy purplish tone. The Aboriginal
name is "Katajuta," meaning "mountain of many heads."*

Left:
THE DEVIL'S MARBLES, NORTHERN TERRITORY
The Devil's Marbles, described by one small child as "giant scones," are a collection of immense round granite boulders. A number are piled one upon another, with crevices between and occasionally cave-like spaces beneath. Others are scattered across the plain, their red colour an effective backdrop to the pure white limbs of the Ghost Gums. Weathering, principally the flaking away of thin flat slabs, has rounded rocks which were initially fractured into rectangular and square blocks.

Above:
AYERS ROCK SUNRISE, NORTHERN TERRITORY
In the distance the huge rock, framed by foreground dead and living Desert Oaks, catches the first rays of sunlight, and for a few minutes glows as if illuminated from within. The colour of the rock, from a distance, changes throughout the day, from glowing pink at sunrise to brick red of sunlit rock, then blue shadows of late afternoon, and finally to black silhouette as the sun nears the far horizon.

117

THE VALLEY OF WINDS,
MOUNT OLGA,
NORTHERN TERRITORY
A narrow gorge between two of the enormous vertical-walled domes of Mount Olga, the Valley of Winds is named for the greatly accentuated strength of wind rushing through the crevice-like gap. The floor of the valley rises steadily, then drops away again towards the other side. From this point there is an impressive view, framed by the vertical cliffs on each side of the Valley of Winds, to the domes at the far end of the mountain.

10 Changed by Man

The wilderness landscape—natural bush country unchanged by man—shows best of all the true face of Australia, but there are many scenes, wholly or partly created by the activities of man, which are quite beautiful. Some are attractive in a placid way, like scenes of contented cattle on lush pastures; others have a disturbing beauty, like the huge gaunt skeletons of ringbarked Karri trees that were killed to provide a few acres of pasture.

In some regions man has been far more sympathetic in his treatment of the environment than elsewhere. But it is more likely than not that the roughness of the terrain, rather than any deliberate thought for conservation of natural resources, prevented him from destructive activities.

The Great Dividing Range is for the most part so mountainous that the steeper hills have been permitted to remain forested, while the lower slopes and valleys have been cleared for agriculture. The country inland from Grafton, along the Boyd River, is one example of this. It retains a balance of steep forested ranges and cleared green river flats, giving a very attractive environment.

In Western Australia's Darling Range large areas have been set aside as State forests, while many valleys, such as the Chittering Valley north of Perth, have been cleared. The intermingling of farms and forests is not only scenically attractive, but makes sound use of both timber and agriculture resources.

Not everywhere has the land been wisely utilised. In some areas excessive clearing and grazing on steep slopes has caused extensive erosion, deep gullies across paddocks, and land rendered useless by salt accumulation. Parts of the steep Flinders Ranges have been grazed until bare of vegetation. In north Queensland patches of rainforest still remain on the more rugged mountain areas, and a few very small areas on the coastal plains, to show the magnificent type of vegetation that once covered most of that region.

Our forests were regarded by early settlers as a hindrance, the popular belief being that the tallest trees grew on the best land. Today there are innumerable eroded hill slopes and abandoned overgrown farms because of this concept. Australia's limited forests need to be preserved, both in forestry reserves and in national parks. Yet even today, despite the ecological mistakes of the past, there is continued clearing of our diminishing forests for agricultural "development," while much of the land already cleared is lying idle or remains only partially productive.

EARLY MORNING CALM, LAKE EILDON, VICTORIA
Lake Eildon is a man-made lake created by the damming of the Goulburn and Delatite Rivers. The area around some of the reservoir's inlets, particularly Coller Bay, is very attractive. New trees are being planted, and half-tame kangaroos in considerable numbers emerge from the bush to feed around the shore in early morning and in the evenings.

Left:
RINGBARKED KARRI FOREST, WESTERN AUSTRALIA
In the south-west of Western Australia the forests of towering Karri trees are the principal natural wonder of the region, a major tourist attraction, and the basis of a timber milling industry. But in the past, and sometimes today, Karri forest has been destroyed to make way for far less valuable activities. Small dairy farms, most failing to provide a reasonable living, are all that we have in large areas where beautiful and valuable Karri trees once grew. The trees were ring-barked so that grass would grow beneath, and the excellent hardwood timber was never utilised.

Above:
BOYD RIVER, NORTH-EASTERN NEW SOUTH WALES
In north-eastern New South Wales the coastal rivers have carved deep valleys and gorges into the eastern escarpment of the Great Dividing Range. The mountain slopes and summits, in places 5,000 feet high, are heavily forested, with rainforest on the wetter parts of the eastern slopes, and eucalypt forests on both lowlands and high tableland areas. This magnificent wilderness scene on the Boyd River, a tributary of the Clarence River, near Grafton, has been changed by man only along the river flats, where small areas have been cleared for grazing.

Left:
CUNNINGHAM'S GAP, GREAT DIVIDING RANGE, QUEENSLAND
Far beyond these ringbarked trees in a paddock near Aratula, Cunningham's Gap, a saddle-shaped pass over the Great Dividing Range, is silhouetted against the sunset. Although the lowlands have been greatly altered by the activities of man, the ranges at Cunningham's Gap have been preserved in natural condition. The Cunningham Highway twists up the range and passes over the top at the lowest part of the saddle. At that point are magnificent views, dense rain-forest, and walking tracks to the summits of the adjacent peaks: Mount Cordeaux and Mount Mitchell.

Above:
CHITTERING VALLEY, WESTERN AUSTRALIA
Winter spreads a carpet of green over paddocks that for much of the year are dry grey-brown in colour. The late afternoon sun, low in the sky, shines through every translucent blade of grass, making the green particularly vivid when seen against the light. The Chittering Valley is an old farming area in the Darling Range about thirty-five miles north of Perth. On the undulating hills around the valley are large areas of Wandoo forest country, where large attractive white-barked trees shelter an undergrowth that has many wildflowers from late winter into spring.

125

THE NANDEWAR RANGE, NORTHERN NEW SOUTH WALES
This valley, hidden in the Nandewar Range of northern New South Wales, is accessible by tortuous winding roads over the mountain; one of these roads passes over the top of Mount Kaputar. The fertile river flats along the floor of the valley and the lower slopes of the hills have been cleared, while the more rugged heights remain forested. These hills are of volcanic origin, with tall rock spires, the remains of old volcanoes, still to be seen in some parts.

BARRAGES, LAKE ALEXANDRINA, SOUTH AUSTRALIA
*Where the Murray enters the sea in South Australia, cliffs have given
way to long sandy beaches and sand dunes. The mouth of the Murray
River is largely blocked by a sand bar that holds the water back in
shallow lakes, Lake Albert, Lake Alexandrina, and the Coorong. It
is on Lake Alexandrina, seven miles from the mouth of the Murray,
near the little township of Goolwa, that this barrage controlling the
river's flow has been built.*